Reading Current Issues: Developing Communication Skills through English

知っておくべき日本と世界の論点・未来の夢

by
Tom Dillon
Koji Nishiya

TSURUMI SHOTEN

自習用音声について

本書の自習用音声は以下より無料でダウンロードできます。予習、復習にご利用ください。
(2020年4月1日開始予定)

http://www.otowatsurumi.com/3883/

URLはブラウザのアドレスバーに直接入力して下さい。
パソコンでのご利用をお勧めします。圧縮ファイル(zip)ですのでスマートフォンでの場合は事前に解凍アプリをご用意下さい。

はしがき

　本教材は、英語そのものを学ぶ教材ではありません。本テキストを使用した授業を通じて、学生の皆さんに最終的に力をつけていただきたいのは「コミュニケーション能力」です。

　「学生の関心事・悩み」についての調査結果を載せているあるウェブサイトによると、就職に関することが第1位になっていますが、それ以外では、友人との人間関係、恋愛、両親とのコミュニケーションなどが上位に来ています。また、経団連の調査でも、面接官が就職時の面接で最も重視するのが「コミュニケーション能力」だと言われています。

　一方で、いじめ、少子高齢化、貧困、災害、地球温暖化、戦争・紛争など、日本と世界には多くの問題が山積しています。これらの問題を解決するためには、問題の原因・背景・歴史と現在の状況をよく知ったうえで、自分の意見・考えをしっかり持ち、相手に伝え、相手の意見・考えをよく聞いて対策を立てて行かなければなりません。大きな問題であっても、解決のためのプロセスで必要なものは「コミュニケーション能力」です。

　本書は、「コミュニケーション能力」を鍛えるために、日本と世界に山積するいろいろなテーマを15ユニット用意しました。ユニット1からユニット12まではどれも私たち自身や日本と世界にとって悩ましい大きな問題です。ユニット13からユニット15は、未来の夢のあるテーマを用意しました。どのユニットにおいても、「よく知って」「よく考えて」「よく感じて」、その上で、自分の意見・考えを相手に伝える練習をしてください。上手い英語でなくても構いません。英語で伝えるのが難しければ、最初は日本語でもいいでしょう。まずは、自分の意見・考えを持って、それを伝える練習をしてください。本テキストに含まれる英文やエクササイズはそのための素材です。少し見慣れない英語の用語があるかもしれませんが、そこでつまずかないように、日本語の説明も豊富に付けました。よく知って、よく調べて、よく考えて、よく聞いて、よく伝えてください。

　本書を執筆するにあたり、大きなテーマを簡潔な英文にまとめていただいたトム・ディロン氏にあらためて心からお礼申し上げます。

2019年11月

著者代表　西谷　恒志

各ユニットの構成と利用法

❏ 日本と世界を取り巻くさまざまな問題・未来の夢

　Unit 1–Unit 12 では、日本と世界を取り巻くさまざまな問題を取り扱います。Unit 13–Unit 15 では、未来に実現可能な人類の夢を取り扱います。

★ タイトル

　タイトルは本文の内容に密接に関連した語句や、内容を数語で凝縮した語句でできています。本文を聞いたり読んだりする前に、必ずタイトルを見て本文のトピックを把握するようご指導ください。

★ リード

　日本語で本文の内容を簡潔にまとめたり、本文のトピックに関する問題提起をしています。本文の内容に関する事前情報を与える役割をしています。この事前情報も本文を理解する上で大変重要です。

★ Pre-Study: Words & Phrases

　各 Unit には、それぞれのトピックに関する専門的な用語や固有名詞が含まれます。これらの語句に加えて、本文の英文のうち比較的難しい語句の意味や補足説明となっています。ここで取り扱う語句を理解した上で、本文の学習に進んでください。

★ 英文

　豊富なジャンルからさまざまなトピックを選びました。どのトピックも大きな問題、あるいは、すばらしい夢のあるトピックです。

　理解しやすいように、各 Unit は 4 つのパラグラフから構成されています。第 1 パラグラフには、多くの場合、本文の主題文（トピックセンテンス）が入っています。特に第 1 パラグラフから本文の主題文を読み取るようご指導ください。なお、Words & Phrases で説明している語句には薄いグレーのマーカーを付しています。

★ Exercises:

A: Comprehension Questions: 4 問

　原則として、4 つのパラグラフから 1 問ずつ Question を出題しています。

B: Questions for Discussion: 3 問

　本テキストは、「英語で日本と世界を取り巻くさまざまな問題・未来の夢を学ぶ」ことを目的にしています。このエクササイズで重要なことは、問題点（論点）を捉えること、感じる

こと、考えること、相手に伝えることです。3問は英語で与えられていますが、すべて英語で答えなくても構いません。難しい場合は、日本語で答えても構いません。A. 〜 D. の4つの選択肢がありますが、自分の考えが4つの選択肢以外であっても構いません。

★ Typical Expressions for Communication:
　　Exercises, B の回答に役に立つ表現を15項目でまとめました。どれも基本的なものばかりです。また、取り上げた表現以外にも数多くの表現があります。各自調べて、表現の引き出しを増やすようご指導ください。

CONTENTS

はしがき
各 Unit の構成と利用法

Unit 1　**Communication** 1

Unit 2　**Inflation or Deflation** 6

Unit 3　**Pension Plans in Japan** 11

Unit 4　**Microplastics** 16

Unit 5　**Global Warming** 21

Unit 6　**Thinking About Poverty** 26

Unit 7　**China: Today and Tomorrow** 31

Unit 8　**Population Decline and Foreign Workers** 36

Unit 9　**Work Style Reform and Productivity** 41

Unit 10　**Bullying in School** 46

Unit 11　**Armed Conflicts and Refugees** 51

Unit 12　**Food Waste** 56

Unit 13　**Future Energy** 61

Unit 14　**Medical Care in the Future** 66

Unit 15　**The Universe in the Future** 71

UNIT 1
Communication

「学生の関心事・悩み」についての調査結果を載せているあるウェブサイトによると、就職に関することが第1位になっている。だが、それ以外では、友人との人間関係、恋愛、両親とのコミュニケーションなどが上位に来ている。経団連の調査でも、面接官が就職時の面接で最も重視するのが「コミュニケーション能力」だという。"コミュニケーション"は、大学生の最大の関心事・悩みのようだ。

Pre-Study: Words & Phrases

line
- 3 **... is followed in rapid order by *A*, *B*, and *C*** 「…のすぐ後に順に続くのは*A*、*B*、そして*C*である」
- 4 **(the) Japanese Business Federation cites *A* as *B*** 「経団連：日本経済団体連合会は*A*を*B*として挙げている」
- 5 **communicative competence** 「コミュニケーション能力」
- 5 **the most critical asset** 「最も重要な資質」
- 6 **potential job seekers** 「将来性のある就職希望者」
- 8 **the Tokyo Advertising Association** 「(公益社団法人)東京広告協会」
- 11 **lessen the social gap** 「つきあいにおけるギャップを減少させる」
- 17 **the foundation of** 「～の基本」
- 20 **patience** 「我慢(強さ)、忍耐」
- 25 **by striving to communicate with** 「～とコミュニケーションをしようと懸命に努力することによって」

UNIT 1

1 A website focusing on the concerns and interests of Japanese young people lists the top worry of Japanese youths as being their future job, according to a survey. This is followed in rapid order by concerns about relationships with friends, romance, and communicating with parents. A study by the Japanese Business Federation cites communicative competence during the interview process as being the most critical asset for potential job seekers. All things considered, it seems that communication should be the largest concern of university students today.

2 A Tokyo Advertising Association survey of one thousand university students found that 52% feel that their personality changes according to whom they are with and the group they are in at the moment. They adjust their personalities in order to smooth over relationships and lessen the social gap with people they are with. Such adjustment also allows them to establish their own position within the group. This survey also shows how much university students struggle with communication.

3 How does a person become talented in communication? Basically, good communication means correctly understanding the words and thoughts of other individuals, while at the same time also expressing one's own true feelings and thoughts. Yet what is the foundation of communicative competence?

4 The answer is "listening." To communicate well, a person must first listen to everything the other individual has to say. This may seem simple, but it requires a great deal of patience. Most people believe they have already understood and often interrupt other speakers. Yet it is important to wait until the other person has finished before commenting or asking questions. The ability to listen well to the very end does not develop overnight, but it is a necessary skill for building strong relationships with friends, co-workers, and family members. Communicative competence can be acquired only by striving to communicate with the people around us day by day.

(313 words)

Exercises

A Comprehension Questions

1. According to the text, what skill do job seekers need most?

   A. The ability to work in rapid order
   B. The ability to take surveys
   C. The ability to communicate during interviews
   D. The ability to make critical assessments

2. Why do university students adjust their personalities according to those they are with?

   A. They hope for jobs in advertising.
   B. Surveys show that 52% of the people they are with cannot communicate.
   C. They hope to make personal relationships go better.
   D. They are unhappy with the groups they are in.

3. According to the text, what are the two elements of good communication?

   A. Understanding well and expressing oneself
   B. Being talented and patient
   C. Having feelings and thoughts
   D. Smoothing relationships and reducing distance from others

4. According to the text, what do poor listeners often do?

   A. Listen to the very end
   B. Listen all night
   C. Adopt a simple approach to communication
   D. Interrupt before the other speakers finish

UNIT 1

B Questions for Discussion

次の 1.〜3. の質問について「自分がもっとも同意できる考え」を選択肢 A.〜D. より選び、選択した理由を具体的に述べなさい。

1. Who do you feel is more difficult to communicate with?

    A. My girlfriend/boyfriend because I always hope to impress her/him.
    B. My parents because they do not understand the younger generation.
    C. The co-workers at my part-time job because the only shared interest we have is our work.
    D. My friends because they have too many worries of their own.

    ....
    ....
    ....

2. What do you feel about the survey results stating that 52% of Japanese university students adjust their personalities according to those they are with?

    A. It shows the relationship pressure that students feel.
    B. This is a very normal thing to do and is hardly worth mentioning.
    C. The 48% who do not adjust are the ones who are strange. Adjusting is critical for communication.
    D. It shows that society is expecting too much from young people today.

    ....
    ....
    ....

3. Do you agree that communication begins with good listening?

    A. Yes, one cannot communicate without understanding others.
    B. Yes, but it is a two-way street. If one person listens well and the other does not, communication will fail.
    C. No. Look at texting* and chat rooms. Users have lots of time to read over and think about other people's comments, but they still get excited and miscommunicate.
    D. No, the most important thing is truly wanting to understand the other person. Listening well is only part of that.

Notes: texting「携帯電話などのテキストメッセージの送受信」

....
....
....

Typical Expressions for Communication:
感じたこと、思ったことを伝えよう①

〈肯定的な感情〉

be happy:
I'm so happy to hear that.
（それを聞いてとてもうれしい。）

be glad:
I'm glad to see you.
（きみに会えてうれしい。）

be delighted:
I'm delighted that you can stay one more night.
（きみがもう一晩いることができてとてもうれしい。）

be pleased:
I'm really pleased that he's feeling better.
（彼の具合が良くなってきているのでとてもうれしい。）

be satisfied:
I'm very satisfied with my score in math.
（数学の試験の点数にはとても満足している。）

UNIT 2
Inflation or Deflation

インフレとデフレは私たちの生活にどのような影響を与えるのか？ インフレになると、物価は上がる、つまり、貨幣（お金）価値が低下する。一方、デフレーションとはこの逆に、「モノやサービスの価格が下がること」である。これは同時に「貨幣の価値が上がること」を意味している。2012年から始まったいわゆる「アベノミクス」と称される経済政策を背景とした日本の現状と私たちの生活をあらためて考えてみる。

Pre-Study: Words & Phrases

line
2 **monetary value**「貨幣価値」
5 **a manageable inflation rate**「管理可能なインフレ率」
7 **set out to conquer deflation**「デフレを克服することを始めた」
8 **quantitative-qualitative easing**「量的・質的金融緩和」（金融政策の対象を資金供給量に変更し、「質」としては長期国債や投資信託などの買入れ額を拡大）
9 **government bonds**「国債」
10 **has been dubbed "Abenomics"**「アベノミクスと称されている」（アベノミクス：第二次安倍内閣が掲げた一連の経済政策で、インフレターゲットの設定と大胆な金融緩和を特長とする。）
11 **savings**「貯蓄」
13 **1,829 trillion yen**「1,829兆円」
14 **17 trillion US dollars**「17兆ドル」
17 **far more prone to invest in**「〜に投資するする傾向がはるかに強い」
18 **susceptible to inflation**「インフレに影響されやすい」
19 **inflation resistant**「インフレに対する抵抗力がある」

How do inflation and deflation affect our lives? Inflation causes increased prices for goods and services. It also means loss of monetary value. Deflation is the exact opposite. The price of goods and services go down and the value of money goes up.

 So, why do people in the government always say that deflation is undesirable and we need a manageable inflation rate instead? Inflation means a rise in the cost of living, meaning that the value of money drops. How can that be positive? Yet, beginning in 2012, the second Abe Administration set out to conquer deflation by establishing inflation targets and setting a bold monetary policy of quantitative-qualitative easing, which basically means that the Bank of Japan would purchase government bonds and other assets in order to feed the economy. This approach has been dubbed "Abenomics."

 The disadvantage of inflation can be seen from a look at Japanese savings. From January to March in 2018, Japanese household assets totaled roughly 1,829 trillion yen, or over 17 trillion US dollars. Of this amount approximately 52% consisted of cash or bank deposits. In comparison, only 13% of American household assets are in cash or bank deposits, while in Europe the figure is 33%. Households in the United States and Europe are far more prone to invest in stocks or bonds than households in Japan. This means Japanese households are very susceptible to inflation while American and European households are more inflation resistant.

 What happens with deflation? If the cost of living does not rise, corporations will have limited profits and will not be able to grow and develop. Furthermore, the value of corporate assets will slowly shrink. In such an environment, it is easy for businesses to fail, even if they borrow money and invest. The merits and demerits of inflation versus deflation can thus change according to one's point of view. Saying that both are bad is just too simple.

(321 words)

UNIT 2

Exercises

A Comprehension Questions

1. What happens to goods and services during deflation?

    A. They become exact opposites.

    B. They become more expensive.

    C. They get cheaper.

    D. They drop in value.

2. What seems to be a key feature of the economic strategy of the second Abe Administration?

    A. Increasing deflation

    B. Applying the name Abenomics

    C. Ensuring that the value of money continues to rise

    D. Using government funds to stimulate the economy

3. Why are Japanese families more likely to suffer from inflation than families in the United States or Europe?

    A. Because Japanese families keep more assets in cash

    B. Because Japanese families must deal with Abenomics

    C. Because Japanese families have very little savings

    D. Because Japanese families keep their savings inside their houses

4. How might deflation affect a corporation?

    A. It will reduce a corporation's opportunities to invest.

    B. It will increase corporate assets.

    C. It will increase corporate investments.

    D. It will create a healthy environment for borrowing money.

B Questions for Discussion

次の 1.～3. の質問について「自分がもっとも同意できる考え」を選択肢 A.～D. より選び、選択した理由を具体的に述べなさい。

1. Why do Japanese families keep a high percentage of their assets in cash?

    A. Most families are unfamiliar with investment strategies and opportunities.
    B. Families look upon stocks and bonds as risky.
    C. Cash assets are easier to use in an emergency.
    D. Families rarely communicate about financial planning for the future and move ahead only one day at a time.

    ....
    ....
    ....

2. Which is preferable, inflation or deflation?

    A. Inflation, because if the cost of living goes up, so will salaries.
    B. Inflation, because higher profits will mean more jobs.
    C. Deflation, because prices will remain low.
    D. Deflation, because while inflation may help large companies, it hurts individuals.

    ....
    ....
    ....

3. Have the Abenomics reforms been successful?

    A. It is too early to tell.
    B. No, the economy today seems almost the same as the economy prior to Abenomics.
    C. Yes, the Japanese economy has slowly been revitalized.
    D. Perhaps, but outside factors, such as trade tensions with other countries, are causing obstacles.

    ....
    ....

Typical Expressions for Communication:
感じたこと、思ったことを伝えよう②

〈否定的な感情〉

be shocked:
I'm shocked to hear that he has resigned.
　（彼が辞職したことを聞いて驚いています。）

be anxious:
I'm anxious about my relationship with friends.
　（友人との関係について心配している。）

be angry:
I was very angry with myself for making such a mistake.
　（そんな間違いをして自分自身にとても腹が立った。）

be sad:
I was sad that he had to leave this morning.
　（彼が今朝出発しなければならないので悲しかった。）

UNIT 3
Pension Plans in Japan

公的年金制度は、「国が行う年金制度」であり、それには、社会保障の観点から財政援助と税制優遇措置が伴う。年金は加入者が65歳になると支給が開始され、終身継続する。年金支給のための財源は賦課方式というもので、現役世代が納める保険料がそのときの年金受給者への支払いに充てられる。だが、日本の人口は減り続けており、2050年には現役のほぼ1人が1人の年金を賄わなければならなくなる。年金制度は大きな問題を抱えている。

Pre-Study: Words & Phrases

line
1 **is administered by**「～によって運営されている」
2 **furnishes a lifetime pension**「終身年金を提供する」
6 **equivalent to saving**「貯蓄と同等で」
8 **susceptible to**「～の影響を受けやすい」
9 **"pay-as-you-go" method**「賦課方式」(現役世代が"現金を支払って"年金受給世代を助ける方式)
14 **an adequate number of contributors**「十分な数の(年金)拠出者」
17 **As of 2015**「2015年現在」
18 **lifespans**「寿命」
19 **predictions**「予測」
20 **ratio**「比率、割合」
20 **disastrous results**「悲惨な結果」
24 **in need of reform**「改革の必要がある」

UNIT 3

🎧 9 The Japanese national pension system is administered by the government and provides financial support for retired citizens. The system furnishes a lifetime pension for retired individuals, basically according to how much money each person paid into the system. Such pensions begin at age sixty-five and provide cost-of-living support for elderly people who can no longer work.

🎧 10 Contributing to one's national pension is equivalent to saving for one's future. The amount each individual contributes will one day come back. However, such savings are susceptible to inflation. Amounts contributed today will not have the same buying power in the future. Japanese government pensions thus adopt a "pay-as-you-go" method, in which contributions from the current working generation are used to help fund the pensions of older generations. The merit of this method is that it adjusts according to inflation. If the cost of living should rise, both pensions and contributions increase. The pension system is thus very stable.

🎧 11 Yet for the system to work, there must be an adequate number of contributors from the current working generation. If the number of contributors should drop, supporting retired people becomes questionable, with the only options being to either lower pension amounts or increase contributions. As of 2015, about 2.3 contributors existed for each person in retirement. However, declining birthrates and increased lifespans are changing this. According to some predictions, by the year 2050, there will be only 1.3 contributors for each retired person. Such a ratio would have disastrous results. Individuals aged fifty-five would receive 2.0 to 2.3 times the amount of contributions they paid, but people aged twenty-five would only receive 1.6 to 1.8 times the amount of their contributions.

🎧 12 Considering these factors, the pension system is in need of reform. No matter the shape of such reform, living comfortably on a Japanese national pension alone may be difficult. People need to plan for their old age while still young. At the same time there is a growing gap between rich and poor, with some people due to receive small pensions and others none at all. How to handle the pension situation has thus become a political issue in Japan.

(356 words)

Exercises

A Comprehension Questions

1. When do Japanese people begin receiving their Japanese national pension?

    A. Once they begin making contributions

    B. All their lives

    C. As soon as they stop working

    D. From age sixty-five

2. What is one key advantage of the Japanese pension system?

    A. Older generations help support younger ones.

    B. The system adapts according to inflation.

    C. Pension values decline over time.

    D. There is no gap between rich and poor.

3. What is the problem in the pay-as-you-go system?

    A. It does not consider inflation.

    B. The declining birthrate is decreasing the number of active workers.

    C. It calls for lower contributions and higher pensions.

    D. Fewer people will soon be needed to support the elderly.

4. When does the text suggest it is best to begin preparing for retirement?

    A. At age sixty-five

    B. In the year 2050

    C. When still young

    D. After retirement

B Questions for Discussion

次の 1. ~ 3. の質問について「自分がもっとも同意できる考え」を選択肢 A. ~ D. より選び、選択した理由を具体的に述べなさい。

1. What is most frustrating about the Japanese pension system?

    A. Working people have to sacrifice their income to pay for other people.
    B. People who have worked hard all their lives are not receiving pensions adequate enough to support them.
    C. Wealthy contributors will receive higher pensions than poorer people. Wealth is not an indicator of how hard one has worked in one's life.
    D. The Japanese government is taking so many years to try to solve the problem.

    ....
    ....
    ....

2. If a person's pension is not enough to support him or her, what might happen to such a person?

    A. Their only option is to continue to hunt for work long after age sixty-five.
    B. Homelessness and crime are unfortunate possibilities.
    C. They must depend on welfare, which comes out of everyone's taxes.
    D. They might suffer from depression, the treatment of which will be paid for with public taxes.

    ....
    ....
    ....

3. Is there any hope for the current Japanese pension system?

    A. Yes. Introducing more foreign workers would bring more contributors.
    B. Yes. If the economy grows, everyone will have more money to spend and contribute.
    C. No. Reform must begin with removal of the leadership that created the system.
    D. No. People would do better by saving and investing on their own.

    ....

....
....

Typical Expressions for Communication:
感じたこと、思ったことを伝えよう③

〈「確信・自信」の表現〉

I believe ... :
I don't believe what you're saying to me.
（きみがぼくにいま言っていることが信じられない。）

I'm sure ... :
I'm pretty sure that she'll agree.
（きっと彼女は賛成すると思う。）

I'm confident ... :
I'm confident that she will pass the exam.
（きっと彼女は試験に合格すると思う。）

I'm convinced ... :
I am convinced that we are on the right track.
（我々は正しい道を進んでいると私は確信している。）
＊信じる度合いが強い言い方

UNIT 4
Microplastics

マイクロプラスチックは 5mm より小さい微粒子のプラスティックで、近年特に海洋環境において極めて大きな問題となっている。マイクロプラスチックに関するある世界分布モデルでは、約5兆個のマイクロプラスチックが世界の海を漂っている。レジ袋の有料化やプラスティック製ストローの廃止など、マイクロプラスチックの発生源を減らす取り組みが世界中で増えているのには、このような背景がある。

Pre-Study: Words & Phrases

line
1　**fine particles**「微粒子」
1　**the National Oceanic and Atmospheric Administration**「米国海洋大気庁」
6　**microbeads**「マイクロビーズ」(洗顔料・化粧品などに研磨剤として使われる微細なプラスチック粒子)
6　**scrubbing agents associated with**「〜に結びついているスクラブ剤(研磨剤)」
8　**polyethylene terephthalate**「ポリエチレンテレフタラート (PET)」
10　**synthetic fibers**「合成繊維」
11　**fabrics**「布(地)」
11　**sewage water**「下水」
14　**the annual World Economic Forum in Davos**「ダボス会議」(スイスのダボスで開かれる世界経済フォーラムの年次総会。各国の政治家・実業家・専門家が集まり、経済や環境問題を討議する。)
17　**distribution model**「分布モデル」
18　**more than five trillion microplastic particles drifting**「5兆個以上のマイクロプラスチックが漂っている」
21　**are ... ingested by**「〜によって取り込まれる」
21　**accumulate**「蓄積する」
22　**adverse effects**「有害作用」

Microplastics

🎧 13 Microplastics are fine particles of plastic, defined by the National Oceanic and Atmospheric Administration as any piece of plastic of five millimeters in size or smaller. In recent years, microplastics have attracted much attention for their role in harming the environment, especially in polluting the seas.

🎧 14 Although microplastics can be produced in various ways, there are three main sources. First are "microbeads," which are tiny pieces of plastic used in scrubbing agents associated with facial cleansers and cosmetic products. Next are bottles made from polyethylene terephthalate—commonly called PET bottles—and plastic shopping bags from stores. These turn to microplastic particles due to the power of ocean waves and ultraviolet light from the sun. Last are synthetic fibers washed out from fabrics. These fibers enter sewage water and gradually flow into rivers and eventually the sea. According to data from the Ministry of the Environment, over eight million tons of plastic garbage is being released into the world's oceans every year. At the annual World Economic Forum in Davos it was announced that by the year 2050 the volume of microplastics in the sea will be greater than the volume of fish.

Sea area	pieces / km^2
East Asian seas	1,720,000
North Pacific	105,100
world oceans	63,320
Seto Inland Sea	76,000

Table: Comparison of total particle counts computed in four areas.
Data from: Isobe et al.(2016); Eriksen et al.(2014)

 15 A world distribution model presented in 2014 by various researchers shows there are more than five trillion microplastic particles drifting in the seas. In fact, the sea near Japan is polluted by microplastics to a level twenty-seven times greater than the world average, according to a study by the Ministry of the Environment. Microplastic particles are then ingested by marine animals and fish and accumulate in their bodies.

 16 Numerous studies have shown the adverse effects of microplastics on marine life. For example, microplastics have been found to cause liver tumors in fish and to reduce the reproduction capacity of oysters. At present there is no evidence that microplastics are dangerous to human life, but many scientists are very concerned and global society is taking measures to prevent the increase of such plastics. In

recent years some stores have begun charging for plastic bags and some restaurants have stopped using plastic straws. Around the world there is a growing movement to limit the sources of microplastics.

(359 words: Not counting a table)

Exercises

A Comprehension Questions

1. What is the definition of "microplastics"?

    A. Plastic particles made from facial scrub, PET bottles or synthetic fibers
    B. Any plastic particles floating in the ocean
    C. Plastic particles of five millimeters in size or smaller
    D. Plastic particles that are not visible to the eye

2. Which of the following is NOT mentioned as a main source of microplastics?

    A. Makeup
    B. Bottled water
    C. Synthetic clothing
    D. Sewage water

3. Which statement best describes the condition of microplastics in the sea near Japan?

    A. Eighty percent of all fish have ingested microplastics.
    B. Microplastic particles are far more common in Japanese waters than in those of other lands.
    C. The ocean near Japan contains over five trillion microplastic particles.
    D. Microplastics are concentrated in Tokyo Bay.

4. What happens if people eat fish that have ingested microplastic?

    A. They might develop tumors.
    B. They may have diminished reproduction ability.
    C. So far, studies have shown no effects.
    D. So far, no one has eaten such fish.

B Questions for Discussion

次の 1.～3. の質問について「自分がもっとも同意できる考え」を選択肢 A.～D. より選び、選択した理由を具体的に述べなさい。

1. What are some ways people might lessen the use of plastic in their daily lives?

    A. They can refuse plastic shopping bags and carry cloth bags for purchases.
    B. They can refuse plastic straws and drink straight from the cup.
    C. They can carry thermos drinks and avoid PET bottles.
    D. They can give up use of cosmetics.

    ....
    ....
    ....

2. Why are the seas near Japan so heavily polluted with microplastics?

    A. Japan is an island nation with a longer coastline than most other countries.
    B. Japanese people rely on plastic products more than other people.
    C. Japanese have poor manners in regard to throwing away trash.
    D. Plastic trash from Korea and China flows naturally toward Japan.

    ....
    ....
    ....

3. Why is microplastic pollution a bigger problem for Japan than many other countries?

    A. As an island nation, Japan is heavily dependent on the sea.
    B. The typical Japanese diet includes lots of fish.
    C. Japanese companies need plastic to survive in the world markets.
    D. Japanese like to vacation in areas with beautiful beaches, such as Okinawa.

    ....
    ....
    ....

Typical Expressions for Communication:
感じたこと、思ったことを伝えよう④

〈「疑問・不信」の表現〉

I doubt (*that*) ...:
I doubt that the existing pension plan will last until 2030.
　（現在の年金制度が 2030 年まで続くとは思えない。）

I am skeptical about [*of*]:
I am skeptical about her chances of winning.
　（彼女が勝つ見込みはないと思う。）

I don't suppose (*that*) ...:
I don't suppose that he will agree.
　（彼が賛成するとは思えない。）

I'm not convinced of [(*that*) ...]:
I'm not convinced the governor will provide leadership.
　（知事がリーダーシップを発揮するとは信じられない。）

UNIT 5
Global Warming

地球は歴史的に気候の温暖化と寒冷化を何度も繰り返してきたが、地球の平均気温は1906年から2005年の100年間で0.74度上昇している。国連や世界のいろいろな調査によれば、地球温暖化はますます進んでいる。この地球温暖化の原因は温室効果ガスで、特に二酸化炭素の影響が大きい。だが、二酸化炭素の排出が多い国の利害がからみ、各国の対策は地球が期待するほど進んでいない。

Pre-Study: Words & Phrases

line
1 **has often fluctuated**「しばしば変動してきた」
2 **the Intergovernmental Panel on Climate Change**「国連気候変動に関する政府間パネル (IPCC)」（気候変化、影響、適応及び緩和方策に関し、科学的、技術的、社会経済学的な見地から包括的な評価を行うことを目的として世界気象機関（WMO）と国連環境計画（UNEP）により設立された組織）＊ panel「専門家集団、委員会」
3 **fortified by findings that ...**「…という調査結果によって（その信頼性が）強化されている」
5 **hints that ...**「that 以下のことを暗示している」
8 **greenhouse gas**「温室効果ガス」
9 **carbon dioxide**「二酸化炭素」
11 **transforming it into**「it（大気）を～に変化させる」
12 **carbon footprint**「二酸化炭素排出量」
表 **tonnes**「メートルトン」(1 tonne=1,000kg；米国以外の表記で、米国では metric ton と表記。)
18 **It goes without saying that ...**「that 以下のことは言うまでもない」
21 **threatening wildlife**「生態系を脅かしている」
22 **have also heightened racial and ethnic tensions among**「～のあいだで民族的また宗教的対立も高めている」
25 **the Paris Climate Accord**「パリ協定」（2015年に採択された、気候変動抑制に関する多国間の国際的な協定）
27 **being adversely affected**「悪影響を被る」

UNIT 5

17
　　The temperature of the earth has often fluctuated throughout history. However, a study by the Intergovernmental Panel on Climate Change (IPCC) has conclusively determined that the world temperature is trending upward, fortified by findings that, in the one-hundred-year period from 1906 to 2005, the average temperature increased by 0.74 degrees. The trend hints that the temperature will continue to rise in the future.

18
　　The IPCC has also concluded that more than 90% of this increase is likely due to the effects of greenhouse gas. There are several types of such gas, but the most damaging to the environment is carbon dioxide, the amount of which has risen dramatically due to elevated consumption of fossil fuels such as coal, oil, and natural gas. Carbon dioxide remains in the atmosphere, transforming it into a greenhouse of sorts, and thereby warming the earth. In 2018, the world carbon footprint—which is the amount of carbon dioxide released into the air—is said to have been 34 billion tons. The leading carbon producer is China at 9.4 billion tons (or 28% of the total), followed by the United States at five billion tons (15%), India at 2.5 billion tons (7.4%) and Russia at 1.6 billion tons (4.6%). In fifth place comes Japan at 1.2 billion tons (3.4%).

Rank	Country	Million tonnes
1	China	9428.7
2	United States	5145.2
3	India	2479.1
4	Russian Federation	1550.8
5	Japan	1148.4
6	Germany	725.7
7	South Korea	697.6
8	Iran	656.4
9	Saudi Arabia	571.0
10	Canada	550.3

Carbon dioxide emissions in 2018
　　　　　Based on data from "BP Statistical Review of World Energy 2019"

19
　　It goes without saying that global warming is having substantial negative effects. According to the IPCC, one such effect includes the melting of polar ice, which has resulted in a rise in seawater levels around the world and the flooding of low-lying areas. Global warming is also damaging ecosystems and threatening wildlife and essential human resources, such as fish supplies. Drought conditions have also

heightened racial and ethnic tensions among groups faced with decreasing water resources.

The Paris Climate Accord of 2015 adopted strong measures to combat global warming. Such cooperation is critical, as areas producing very little carbon dioxide are being adversely affected by faraway countries that produce much more. African droughts are a good example of this. Nations that produce large amounts of carbon dioxide need to study ways to lighten their carbon footprint and thus help lessen the effect of global warming. Global warming affects every nation on earth!

(368 words: Not counting the table)

Exercises

A Comprehension Questions

1. How much has the world temperature risen in the last century?

    A. More than one percent
    B. Close to one percent
    C. Exactly one percent
    D. There has been no change.

2. How much carbon dioxide does Japan produce compared with China?

    A. Approximately one third
    B. Approximately one fifth
    C. Exactly ten percent
    D. Approximately one eighth

3. Which of the following is NOT mentioned as a negative effect of global warming?

    A. Increased tensions between competing groups
    B. Increased low-lying areas
    C. Increased damage to wildlife habitats
    D. Increased seawater levels

4. African droughts are a good example of what phenomenon?

   A. How carbon dioxide can affect areas far from the place it was produced
   B. Racial and ethnic tensions
   C. The Paris Climate Accord of 2015
   D. The melting of polar ice

B Questions for Discussion

次の1.~3.の質問について「自分がもっとも同意できる考え」を選択肢 A.~D. より選び、選択した理由を具体的に述べなさい。

1. What are ways the average person might help fight global warming?

   A. Use public transportation more
   B. Eat more uncooked vegetables and fruit
   C. Boycott companies that produce large amounts of carbon dioxide
   D. Purchase only eco-friendly appliances

   ....
   ....
   ....

2. How might carbon dioxide producing nations help nations that produce little carbon dioxide?

   A. They can increase financial aid to such areas, depending on how much carbon dioxide they produce.
   B. They can lessen immigration restrictions on people from those areas.
   C. They can unify to dramatically decrease carbon dioxide production worldwide.
   D. They can market more eco-friendly products.

   ....
   ....
   ....

3. Which of the negative effects of global warming might harm Japan the most?

   A. The rise of sea levels
   B. A decrease in fish supplies
   C. Increased ethnic and religious tension
   D. Higher daily temperatures

....
....
....

Typical Expressions for Communication:
感じたこと、思ったことを伝えよう⑤

〈「提案・命令」の表現〉

You should ... :
You should stop comparing yourself to others.
　（他人と自分を比較することをやめたほうがいいですよ。）

You ought to do:
You ought to attend the meeting tomorrow.
　（明日の会議に出席したほうがいいですよ。）
　　＊「提案」「推奨」「アドバイス」の表現。

have to do:
I have to finish my homework before going to bed.
　（寝る前に宿題をしなければならない。）
You have to finish your homework before going to bed.
　（きみは寝る前に宿題をしなければだめだ。）
　　＊発言者の《客観的な判断》として、自分、相手、第三者の「義務」を表す言い方。

must:
You must submit this report today.
　（きみは今日このレポートを提出しなければならない。）
I must submit this report today.
　（私は今日このレポートを提出しなければならない。）
　　＊自分、相手、第三者にとって「必要なこと」、「重要なこと」を表す言い方。主語がYouの場合は「命令」を表すことがあり、主語がIの場合は「意志」を表すことがある。

UNIT 6
Thinking About Poverty

OECDによれば、日本は先進国の中で相対的貧困率が世界第3位(15.7%)の貧困国である。「相対的貧困率」とは、先進国の貧困の度合いを示すもので、世帯所得が全世帯の中央値の半分未満である人の比率である。貧困は住居、教育、労働、食生活、結婚、医療など、さまざまな分野に大きな影響を与える。貧困に伴う社会的な不平等をどのようにして減らしていくのかという政策が問われている。

Pre-Study: Words & Phrases

line
1 **the Organization for Economic Cooperation and Development**「経済協力開発機構(OECD)」(ヨーロッパ、北米等の国々を中心とした、国際経済全般について協議することを目的とした国際機関)
2 **Relative Poverty Ratio**「相対的貧困率」
4 **earnings less than half of the median annual income of all households**「全世帯の年間平均所得の半分以下の所得」*median「中央値の、平均の」
10 **poverty line**「貧困線」
12 **the World Bank**「世界銀行」(各国の中央政府または政府から債務保証を受けた機関に対し融資を行う国際機関)
15 **reside in**「に居住する」
15 **sub-Saharan Africa**「サハラ砂漠より南の地域のアフリカ」
17 **in a variety of critical ways**「各種重大な点において」
17 **limiting options for**「～の選択を制限して」
18 **nutrition**「栄養摂取」
20 **scholastic ability**「学力」
24 **cease to be fun**「楽しくなくなる」
26 **a lower sense of self-esteem**「低い自尊心」
30 **lessen the social inequality**「社会的不平等を減らす」

Thinking About Poverty

21 According to the Organization for Economic Cooperation and Development (OECD), Japan ranks second among developed countries in terms of "Relative Poverty Ratio," at 15.7%. The "Relative Poverty Ratio" is a percentage determined by calculating the number of individuals with earnings less than half of the median annual income of all households in the land. Median income of course varies according to the country. In the case of Japan, the median income is 2,400,000 yen per year. Thus, any individual with annual earnings of 1,200,000 yen or less can be considered to live in "relative poverty." Approximately 20 million Japanese—or 15.7% of the population—fall into this category.

Rank	Location	Latest
1	United States	0.178
2	Japan	0.157
3	Italy	0.137
4	Canada	0.124
5	Great Britain	0.111
6	Germany	0.104
7	France	0.083

Relative Poverty Rate among G7 countries (2014–2017)
Source: OECD Social and Welfare Statistics: Income distribution

22 One of the many factors used to determine poverty is the so-called "poverty line," which is the minimum daily income required to purchase life necessities, such as food and clothing. In 2015, the World Bank set the international poverty line at income below $1.90 American dollars per day. As of that year, approximately 10% of the world's population—about 730 million people—is considered to be living beneath the poverty line. About 86% of these individuals reside in areas of sub-Saharan Africa or South Asia.

23 Poverty, of course, impacts lifestyle in a variety of critical ways, limiting options for housing, education, employment, medical care, nutrition, marriage and more. Let's focus on the case of children's education in Japan. Children from low-income families generally show weaker scholastic ability than children from families with higher incomes. This is because poorer families do not have the economic resources to take advantage of the many study opportunities outside of regular classes, such as cram schools or private lessons. Achievement standards can also vary wildly depending on parents and instructors. Education can cease to be fun for poorer

UNIT 6

students who are caught in such situations, leading to lack of motivation, loss of confidence, and a lower sense of self-esteem. These negative factors then build and feed off each other.

Any child can develop, given proper education; they only need support. Even though private sector funding has recently increased, better public understanding is yet necessary in order to attain long-lasting solutions. How to lessen the social inequality caused by poverty remains an important topic for discussion.

(373 words: Not counting the table)

Exercises

A Comprehension Questions

1. How can another nation receive a similar "Relative Poverty Ratio" as Japan, at 15.7%?

   A. They cannot. Income varies according to the nation.
   B. That nation must have an average annual income of 2,400,000 yen per person.
   C. Each individual must match the annual median income of Japan.
   D. The same percentage of individuals must have less than half of the country's median income.

2. According to the World Bank, what percentage of the planet's population is living under the international poverty line?

   A. 15.7%
   B. 10%
   C. 20 million
   D. 86%

3. Why do Japanese children from poorer families have lower academic achievement?

   A. Their families cannot afford education outside of school.
   B. They have inferior medical care and nutrition.
   C. Their parents were also poor students.
   D. They enter school without confidence or motivation.

4. According to the text, what is required to reach long-lasting solutions as to how poverty affects education and social inequality?

    A. Uniform academic standards
    B. Higher income for everyone
    C. Increased public understanding
    D. Less expensive cram schools

B Questions for Discussion

次の 1.～3. の質問について「自分がもっとも同意できる考え」を選択肢 A.～D. より選び、選択した理由を具体的に述べなさい。

1. How might people in Japan help individuals living below the poverty line overseas?

    A. People should donate money to organizations that bring aid to such areas.
    B. Japan should export Japanese products to such areas at reduced prices.
    C. Japanese should send volunteers to help in those places, providing expertise in education, medicine and agriculture.
    D. Japan should do nothing and focus on its own poor people first.

    ....
    ....
    ....

2. What is the best way to improve awareness of poverty overseas?

    A. Japanese television stations should produce more programs about those areas.
    B. Japan should invite people from those places to study and live in Japan.
    C. Japanese schools should emphasize such areas in Social Studies class.
    D. Japanese schools should plan school trips to those places.

    ....
    ....
    ....

UNIT 6

3. Which of the following is the worst outcome of world poverty?

   A. Loss of income due to reduced export opportunities
   B. The rise of terrorism due to unequal lifestyles
   C. The potential for the spread of disease
   D. Fewer opportunities for world travel

....
....
....

Typical Expressions for Communication:
感じたこと、思ったことを伝えよう⑥

〈「評価・価値判断」の表現〉

appreciate:

I appreciate your making time to meet with us this evening.
（今晩私たちに会う時間をおとりいただき、感謝申し上げます。）

value:

I really value him as a teammate.
（彼をチームメートの一人としてとても大切に思います。）

judge:

Judging from her last email, she seems very well.
（この前のメールから判断すると、彼女は元気でいるようだ。）

overestimate:

I actually overestimated your negotiating skills.
（私は実はきみの交渉スキルを過大評価していた。）

UNIT 7
China: Today and Tomorrow

2018年6月に出されたホワイトハウスの報告書において、中国の行為を "theft" とみなすことばが何回も登場している。その表現が適切だとはあまり思えないが、トランプ政権は中国に対して「知的財産を盗み出す中国を看過することはできず、制裁関税で対抗する」という政策を取っている。アメリカと中国との間で行われている貿易戦争にはこのような背景がある。中国の現在と未来を見てみよう。

Pre-Study: Words & Phrases

line
1. **Economic Aggression**「経済侵略」
2. **Threatens the Technologies and Intellectual Property**「テクノロジーと知的財産を脅かす」
3. **theft**「盗人」
5. **confrontation**「対決」
6. **must not be overlooked**「看過すべきではない」
7. **have recently escalated tariffs on**「最近〜に関する関税を段階的に上げた」
7. **tense**「切迫した」
13. **are dubbed "Haigui"**「Haiguiと呼ばれる」(Haigui [hai gúi] の元の意味は「海亀」。海外留学者が海亀のように生まれ故郷に戻ることから名付けられた。)
15. **with many pursuing fields in**「多くの者は〜の分野で従事しながら」
18. **trade friction**「貿易摩擦」
23. **suffer profoundly**「大きな打撃を受ける」
24. **Gini coefficient**「ジニ係数」(社会における所得分配の不平等さを測る指標。所得が均等に分配されているほど0.0に近くなり、所得の格差が大きいほど1.0に近づく。)
27. **supression of the human rights of minorities**「少数民族への人権弾圧」
28. **the Uighur ethnic group**「ウイグル族」(中国の新疆ウイグル自治区に多く住む少数民族の一つ。近年、中国政府による弾圧が世界に報道されているが、中国は内政問題と主張している。)

UNIT 7

In a June 2018 White House report entitled, "How China's Economic Aggression Threatens the Technologies and Intellectual Property of the United States and the World," the word "theft" was used frequently to describe Chinese business activities. Whether or not the usage is accurate, the Trump Administration has adopted a policy of confrontation, stating that China often steals intellectual property through use of industrial spies or cyber-attacks and that this must not be overlooked. Both nations have recently escalated tariffs on each other's imports and the situation remains tense. China's economy has certainly grown rapidly. Let's look at various aspects of the recent growth.

First, the number of Chinese students studying abroad has increased. According to figures from the Chinese government, 610,000 Chinese students studied abroad in 2017. At the same time, the number of students returning to China after a time of studying abroad totaled 480,000. Returning students are dubbed "Haigui" and are then sent throughout the country in order to contribute to China's economic development. Those students remaining overseas are of similar high ability, with many pursuing fields in economics or political science. There is thus a movement toward more and more outstanding Chinese students studying abroad.

Yet China has various other problems, not only trade friction with the United States. For example, it has a housing problem. Over the last ten years, wealthy Chinese have over-invested in apartment buildings, resulting in a reported housing surplus of fifty million units. So many people are in debt due to sinking their money into housing that, if this real estate bubble bursts, both investors and financial institutions will suffer profoundly. Next is the wide gap between rich and poor. The Gini coefficient is often used to indicate wealth distribution within nations. In 2015, China's Gini coefficient was 0.51, second worst in the world. China also has severe problems with air pollution, over-production of steel and concrete, financially-strapped local governments, suppression of the human rights of minorities, such as the Uighur ethnic group, and other concerns as well.

It cannot be denied that China is developing rapidly. Yet, at the same time, it also has multiple problems of a severe nature. Due to China's giant size and international role, its problems are echoing throughout the world. What will happen now with China? This is a question that demands everyone's attention.

(388 words)

Exercises

A Comprehension Questions

1. According to the text, which of the follow is true of the Trump Administration's outlook on China?

    A. It has accused China of growing too rapidly.
    B. It has accused China of confronting the United States.
    C. It has accused China of threatening White House property.
    D. It has accused China of stealing ideas and technology.

2. What do Chinese exchange students typically do upon returning to China?

    A. They study economics or political science.
    B. They are sent to work in outlying areas to assist with China's growth.
    C. They recruit more and more students to study abroad.
    D. They are sent abroad again as "Haigui."

3. What has seemingly caused the Chinese housing problem?

    A. Trade friction with the United States
    B. Over-investment in apartment buildings
    C. A sinking economy
    D. Fifty million homeless people

4. Why are China's problems important to people around the world?

    A. China has lots of available housing.
    B. Other nations have to breathe China's polluted air.
    C. China has a very low Gini coefficient.
    D. China is a large nation with a powerful economy.

UNIT 7

B Questions for Discussion

次の 1.～3. の質問について「自分がもっとも同意できる考え」を選択肢 A.～D. より選び、選択した理由を具体的に述べなさい。

1. If China is stealing technological secrets, what can be done about it?

   A. Other nations should stop accepting Chinese exchange students.
   B. Nations should stop importing Chinese goods and no longer sell to China.
   C. China must be held responsible, as the Trump Administration is saying.
   D. Other nations should use legal means to challenge China.

   ....
   ....
   ....

2. Is the growing number of Chinese exchange students and Chinese tourists in Japan a good thing?

   A. Yes, these visitors help the Japanese economy.
   B. Yes, they promote closer ties between the two countries.
   C. No, they disrespect Japanese culture and encourage crime.
   D. No, their contributions to Japan are only temporary.

   ....
   ....
   ....

3. What might make Japanese students uncomfortable about studying abroad in China?

   A. All the stories about air pollution
   B. Recent controversies involving trade and territorial rights in the Pacific
   C. Uncertainties with China's economy
   D. Chinese suppression of human rights

   ....
   ....
   ....

Typical Expressions for Communication:
感じたこと、思ったことを伝えよう⑦

〈「非難・不賛成・反対」などの表現〉

fault:
It was his fault that his pet cat died.
　（ペットのネコが死んだのは彼のせいだった。）
It was my fault that we missed the train.
　（われわれがその電車に乗りそこなったのは私のせいだった。）
　＊fault を使っているが、ここでは《謝罪》を表している。

have no excuse:
You have no excuse for being late.
　（きみには遅れたことに弁解の余地はないね。）

against:
In general, I'm against dieting.
　（一般的に言ってダイエットをすることに反対だ。）

not agree:
I don't agree with the death penalty.
　（私は死刑には反対だ。）

reject:
Trump has rejected global warming as a "joke."
　（トランプは地球温暖化を"ジョーク"だと言って否定した。）

UNIT 8
Population Decline and Foreign Workers

少子高齢化を背景に、日本政府は数年前に政策を変更し、外国人労働者の受け入れを拡大させる施策をとった。しかし、日本ではすでに約130万人の外国人労働者が働いているという。こうした外国人労働者は、留学生、技能実習生、定住者・永住者、その他の資格で日本に在留しているのだが、外国人労働者に対する深刻な人権侵害は大きな問題となっている。

Pre-Study: Words & Phrases

line
1 **reversed its course**「方針を変更した」
2 **be attributed to**「(原因は) 〜のせいである」
3 **graying of the population**「人口の高齢化」
4 **the Immigration Control and Refugee Recognition Act**「出入国管理法及び難民認定法」(2019年4月1日施行)
4 **revisions**「改正」
7 **ends the ban on immigration to Japan**「日本への移民禁止を終わらせる」
9 **the Ministry of Health, Labor and Welfare**「厚生労働省」
17 **play key roles**「重要な役割を持つ」
19 **internship trainees**「技能実習生」
20 **human rights violations**「人権侵害」
22 **exceed**「を超える」
24 **enroll in language school**「語学学校に入学する」
25 **difficult to bear**「耐えがたい」
27 **withheld payment**「未払い賃金」
30 **reap tuition fees**「授業料を稼ぐ」

Population Decline and Foreign Workers

In 2018, the Japanese government reversed its course and committed to increasing the numbers of foreign workers. This change can be attributed to the nation's declining birthrate and the overall graying of the population. The government revised the Immigration Control and Refugee Recognition Act, with the revisions going into effect in April of 2019. Under this revision, as many as 345,000 foreign workers may be admitted into Japan over the next five years. Some might argue that this effectively ends the ban on immigration to Japan. In truth, large numbers of foreign workers from a wide variety of nations are already working here.

A 2018 survey by the Ministry of Health, Labor and Welfare found approximately 1.28 million foreigners working in Japan, the highest total ever. According to nationality, Chinese workers were most numerous at about 370,000, 29% of the overall total. Chinese were followed by Vietnamese (240,000 or 19%), Filipinos (150,000 or 12%) and Brazilians (120,000 or 9%). The number of Vietnamese had increased by about 70,000 (40%) over the previous year. The number of workers from Nepal also increased dramatically, rising by 16,000 (31%). Foreign employees are now a common sight at convenience stores, restaurants, and construction sites. Such employees already play key roles in the restaurant and construction industries.

(万人、%)

年 年齢	1990 年 (平成 2 年)	2000 年 (平成 12 年)	2014 年 (平成 26 年)	2020 年 (平成 32 年)	2030 年 (平成 42 年)
計	6,384	6,766	6,587	6,589	6,362
15〜29 歳 比率	1,475 (23.1)	1,588 (23.5)	1,106 (16.8)	1,073 (16.3)	1,027 (16.1)
30〜59 歳 比率	4,177 (65.4)	4,260 (63.0)	4,211 (63.9)	4,205 (63.8)	3,894 (61.2)
60〜64 歳 比率	372 (5.8)	426 (6.3)	572 (8.7)	506 (7.7)	607 (9.5)
65 歳以上 比率	360 (5.6)	494 (7.3)	696 (10.6)	805 (12.2)	835 (13.1)

労働力人口の推移

(Source: www.mhlw.go.jp/wp/hakusyo/.../sh0100-05-b1.xls)

Foreigners live in Japan as exchange students, internship trainees, or as short or long term residents. However, human rights violations have become a serious problem. Many foreign workers find their way to Japan by paying a fee to brokers within their home countries. Because this fee may exceed tens of thousands of yen, as high as one or two years of local income, many people borrow that amount. They come to Japan as exchange students, enroll in language school, and then work in industries introduced by the broker. Yet, many find their work environments difficult to bear. Japanese lawyers helping these foreigners state that problems with low wages, withheld payment, long working hours, and power and sexual harassment are common.

Many reasons lay behind these situations. Overseas brokers may be dishonest, language schools may be accepting and enrolling too many students in order to reap tuition fees, and places of employment may be small scale and cannot afford proper payment for all their workers. The declining birthrate and graying of Japanese society are serious problems, but the difficult employment conditions of foreign workers are issues that have to be solved.

(402 words)

Exercises

A Comprehension Questions

1. Why did the government revise the Immigration Control and Refugee Recognition Act?

   A. The old law allowed too many immigrants.
   B. There were already 345,000 foreign workers in Japan.
   C. Japan had a labor shortage due to low birthrates and an aging population.
   D. The revisions postponed the graying of society for five more years.

2. What ethnic group grew most rapidly prior to the 2018 survey?

   A. Nepalese
   B. Chinese
   C. Filipino
   D. Vietnamese

3. How do many foreign workers find work in Japan?

    A. They are introduced by Japanese language schools.

    B. They are introduced by expensive middlemen within their home countries.

    C. They are introduced by exchange students already living in Japan.

    D. They are recruited directly by the companies they will work for.

4. What is the chief reason for the working condition problems that some foreigners find in Japan?

    A. The revised Immigration Control and Refugee Recognition Act

    B. Dishonest overseas brokers

    C. It is difficult to pinpoint one particular cause.

    D. Dishonest Japanese language schools

B Questions for Discussion

次の 1. ～ 3. の質問について「自分がもっとも同意できる考え」を選択肢 A. ～ D. より選び、選択した理由を具体的に述べなさい。

1. What is the most important requirement for foreigners wishing to work in Japan?

    A. That they be honest and be willing to work hard

    B. That they show respect for Japanese language and customs

    C. That they promise to return to their homelands once their work contracts are concluded

    D. That they use their earnings to purchase Japanese products

    ....
    ....
    ....

2. Why did the government wait so long before relaxing the immigration restrictions?

    A. The Japanese have a reluctance to interact with foreigners.

    B. The government felt the birthrate might rise again.

    C. The government did not want to hand over jobs to foreigners that Japanese might take.

    D. There were no institutions to handle an increase in foreign workers.

UNIT 8

....
....
....

3. If foreign workers have difficulty in the workplace, what course of action should they take?

   A. They need to protest using appropriate legal means.
   B. They should return to their home countries.
   C. They should refuse to work until their demands are met.
   D. They should switch to new jobs as soon as possible.

....
....
....

Typical Expressions for Communication:
感じたこと、思ったことを伝えよう⑧

〈相手に意見を尋ねる；確認する〉

What do you think about ...?:
What do you think about his idea?
　（彼の考えをどう思いますか？）

Do you have any comments about [on] ...?:
Do you have any comments on my views on global warming?
　（地球温暖化に関する私の見方について何かコメントはありませんか？）

Do you have anything to say about ...?:
Do you have anything to say about the construction of the freeway?
　（高速道路の建設について何か意見はありませんか？）

Do you mean to say ...?:
Do you mean to say you're not coming tomorrow?
　（あなたは明日は来ないとおっしゃるのですね？）
　＊相手に《自分の理解》を伝えて確認する表現。

UNIT 9
Work Style Reform and Productivity

ここ数年、日本では「働き方改革」が話題になっている。実際に、日本の労働者が取得する有給休暇日数は、1年間で2週間程度であり、欧米の20日から30日と比べ非常に少ない。だが、もし単純に休暇日数を増やしたり、休暇取得率を上げると、労働生産性が当然下がるが、日本の労働生産性は先進国の中で最下位である。では、どのようにすれば労働生産性が上がるのだろうか。

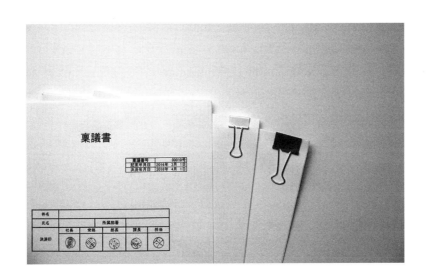

Pre-Study: Words & Phrases

line
- 1 **work style reform**「働き方改革」
- 8 **labor productivity**「労働生産性」
- 表 **GDP (PPP)**「国内総生産 (PPP ベース)」(PPP: Purchasing Power Parity「購買力平価」ベースとは、各国の物価水準の差を修正した、より実質的な値)
- 18 **overdo**「をやりすぎる、を過剰に行う」
- 21 **corporate decision-making**「企業の意思決定」
- 21 **inordinate**「過度の、法外な」
- 25 **out-produce**「を生産で追い抜く」
- 31 **ingenuity**「創意工夫」
- 31 **artificial intelligence**「人工知能 (AI)」
- 33 **result**「(結果として) 起こる、生じる」

UNIT 9

Over the last few years, work style reform has become a topic of keen interest in Japan. The typical Japanese paid leave of two weeks per year is dramatically beneath western totals of twenty to thirty days. Furthermore, only 50% of Japanese employees take all of their paid leave, as opposed to 80% in America. In many countries, such as France and Spain, workers take 100% of their paid holidays, which emphasizes the difference with Japan even more.

Yet, increasing the number of paid holidays and the percentage of workers who take them might result in a sudden loss of labor productivity. The question thus becomes, "Is Japanese labor productivity high enough to allow a somewhat lower level?" Japanese labor productivity currently lists as only two-thirds of that of the United States, with Japanese productivity measured at $47.5 per hour and American productivity at $72 per hour. The Japanese figure is the lowest among the seven most advanced economies of the world. What is more, this is not a new phenomenon. Japanese productivity has had similar ranking since 1970. Therefore, if paid holidays increased and more Japanese workers took them, it is highly probable that production would drop even further, perhaps even resulting in lower salaries.

Rank	Country	GDP(PPP) per hour 2017	Rank	Country	GDP(PPP) per hour 2017
1	Ireland	97.5	11	Australia	64.7
2	Luxembourg	94.7	12	Sweden	62.4
3	Norway	82.3	13	Iceland	62.2
4	Belgium	73.5	14	Finland	59.7
5	Denmark	72.2	15	Australia	57.6
6	United States	72.0	16	Italy	55.5
7	Germany	69.8	17	Spain	53.8
8	Netherlands	69.3	18	Canada	53.7
9	Switzerland	68.0	19	United Kingdom	53.5
10	France	67.8	20	Japan	47.5

Labor Productivity per Hour

Source: OECD 2017

What are the reasons behind Japan's low labor productivity? One thought is that the service industry is overdoing it, providing services beyond what is necessary. On the one hand, offering excellent service is the best way to treat customers and clients, but such service also results in increased hours for workers. Another reason might be that Japanese corporate decision-making is said to take an inordinate amount of time. Individuals in positions of authority are thought to be weak, with even the slightest moves needing approval from various bosses and section chiefs. One further reason is increased economic competition with other countries in Asia. Japan has to strive hard to out-produce its competitors.

How can Japan increase its labor productivity? When it comes to decision-making, many feel more authority should be given to the individuals in charge of each section. This would certainly speed up work processes and save time, resulting in better production in many areas. As to work style reform, Japanese employees need to take more of their paid leave, whether or not the amount is increased. If labor production rises due to better ingenuity, the added application of artificial intelligence, more efficient use of labor, including the end to excessive service, then taking time off would become more natural and shorter work hours would result.

(423 words: Not counting the table)

Exercises

A Comprehension Questions

1. How much more of their paid holidays do workers in France take in comparison with workers in Japan?

   A. 100%
   B. 80%
   C. 67%
   D. 50%

2. How long has Japanese work productivity ranked low, as compared with other advanced economies of the world?

   A. Since the turn of the century
   B. For almost half a century
   C. Only in recent years
   D. Since other Asian economies became more competitive

UNIT 9

3. Which of the following is NOT given as a reason for Japan's low work productivity?

    A. The low amount of paid holidays
    B. Poor corporate decision-making
    C. Competition from nearby countries
    D. Going to extremes in offering service

4. According to the text, how can Japan companies improve decision-making?

    A. Each boss and section chief needs to be more involved.
    B. All individuals in positions of responsibility need more paid vacations.
    C. Employees need more authority to make decisions on the spot.
    D. Japanese companies need to offer more services.

B Questions for Discussion

次の1.～3.の質問について「自分がもっとも同意できる考え」を選択肢A.～D.より選び、選択した理由を具体的に述べなさい。

1. Why don't Japanese workers take all of their paid holidays?

    A. They feel pressure from their companies to remain at work.
    B. Many men feel more comfortable in the workplace than at home with their families.
    C. Everyone's paid holidays tend to fall at the same time, making transportation and lodging expensive and crowded.
    D. Workers might lose overtime opportunities and most people need that extra income.

    ....
    ....
    ....

2. Should the Japanese service industry cut back on services?

    A. No. Japanese service is the best in the world.
    B. No. That would cause Japan to lose in competition with foreign firms.
    C. Yes. Japanese companies provide too much service.
    D. Yes. That might result in lower prices and increase the number of customers.

....
....
....

3. What is the best way to improve corporate decision-making?

   A. Employees should specialize more and not transfer around to various units of the company.
   B. Lifetime employment must end. If leaders cannot raise company profits, then they need to be let go and replaced.
   C. Japanese companies should hire more foreign administrators who know how to be productive even with lots of paid holiday time.
   D. Japanese companies should have fewer meetings and just let the bosses decide everything.

....
....
....

Typical Expressions for Communication:
感じたこと、思ったことを伝えよう⑨

〈「推測・可能性」を表す表現〉

It is likely that ...:
It is likely that food waste collection will be required for large businesses.
　（食品廃棄物の収集は大企業に求められているようだ。）

may [might] do:
You may already know about food waste.
　（食品破棄についてはもう知っているかもしれませんね。）

It is possible that ...:
It is possible that reducing household food waste may be important.
　（家庭の食品廃棄物を減らすことが重要なのかもしれない。）

not certain:
The troubles are not certain to be solved quickly.
　（その問題がすぐに解決されるかどうかは確かでない。）

UNIT 10
Bullying in School

現在、世界中で「いじめ」が満ちあふれている。子どもが子どもに行ういじめ、親が子どもに行う児童虐待、夫が妻に行う DV、職場で上司が部下に行う各種ハラスメント、などである。こうした中、「学校におけるいじめ」は強い関心の的となっている。日本では長年、いじめをなくすために「いじめる行為はよくない」という道徳的なアプローチを採用してきたが、根本的な解決に大きな効果をもたらしたとは言えない状況だ。

Pre-Study: Words & Phrases

line
- 1 **bully**「をいじめる；いじめっ子」
- 2 **spouses**「配偶者」
- 3 **harass**「に嫌がらせをする、を困らせる」
- 4 **intense**「強烈な、激しい」
- 5 **the Ministry of Education, Culture, Sports, Science and Technology**「文部科学省」
- 10 **prolonged absences**「長期欠席」
- 13 **rise above others**「他の人より優位にいる」
- 14 **assess themselves as**「自分自身を〜と評価する」
- 17 **be left out**「無視される」
- 21 **taking the ethical stance that ...**「…という道徳的な立場を取って」
- 23 **Manabu Wakuta**「和久田学」(公益社団法人子どもの発達科学研究所　主席研究員、大阪大学大学院連合小児発達科学研究科　特任講師)
- 24 **a behavioral science approach**「行動科学的アプローチ」
- 25 **"Be a Hero" project**「"Be a Hero" プロジェクト」(元プロ野球選手の岩隈久志氏を発起人に、公益社団法人 子どもの発達科学研究所、IWA JAPAN、B-creative agency が中心となって立ち上げた活動で、「科学でいじめのない世界を創る」をコンセプトにしている。)
- 27 **coaching victims that ...**「(いじめの) 犠牲者に…ということを指導する」
- 30 **in an objective manner**「客観的なやり方で」

Bullying in School

🎧 37 The modern world is full of cruel relationships. Children bully other children. Parents abuse their children. Spouses commit acts of domestic violence upon their partners. Workplace supervisors harass those beneath them in a variety of ways. And on and on. Among these, school bullying often draws intense attention.

🎧 38 A 2017 study on school bullying by the Ministry of Education, Culture, Sports, Science and Technology found 63,000 cases of violence in elementary, junior high and senior high schools, an increase of 6.5% over the previous year. There were also 410,400 cases of bullying across elementary, junior high and senior high levels, including special classes for the handicapped. This was a one-year increase of 28%. The same study found 210,700 students with prolonged absences and 144,000 students who had dropped out.

🎧 39 In analyzing the psychology of students who commit such bullying, generally three reasons can be given for their actions. First is the desire to rise above others. Typically bullies assess themselves as poor in the areas that most children value, such as being good at studies, sports, television games, and making many friends. This frustration builds until the bully then strikes out at others. The second reason is that bullies hope to be considered part of the group and do not wish to be left out. If someone else is forced from the group, the bully's own position becomes more secure. The third reason is the desire for control, in other words, the desire for power. If the other person shows that they have power too, the bullying stops.

🎧 40 Japan has analyzed bullying in this manner for a number of years, taking the ethical stance that bullying must be stopped. However, it cannot be said that this has brought about a fundamental solution to the problem. Manabu Wakuta, a special lecturer at Osaka University Graduate School, has developed a behavioral science approach to the issue of bullying with his "Be a Hero" project. Wakuta's idea is to encourage students to reach out to bullied classmates and support them, while at the same time coaching victims that it is okay to seek help. This approach teaches children correct behavior and is now being developed at elementary and junior high schools across the land. Under this method, both those who commit acts of bullying and those who suffer from bullying are taught proper behavior in an objective manner. Rather than scold inappropriate behavior, Wakuta's approach is to reward and encourage students when their actions are good. This, everyone hopes, will prevent future acts of bullying.

(427 words)

UNIT 10

Exercises

A Comprehension Questions

1. Which relationship problem is NOT mentioned in the text?

    A. School children harming their classmates
    B. Teachers bullying students
    C. Husbands striking their wives
    D. Bosses harassing employees

2. How much did bullying increase in one year alone?

    A. By 6.5%
    B. By 28%
    C. By 63,000 cases
    D. By 410,400 cases

3. Which is NOT mentioned as a root cause of school bullying?

    A. The desire to be the center of attention
    B. The desire to rise above others
    C. The desire to secure position within the group
    D. The desire for power

4. Which of the following best fits Manabu Wakuta's approach to decreasing the amount of bullying?

    A. Rewarding those who bully others
    B. Rewarding those who are bullied
    C. Rewarding those who help bullied individuals
    D. Rewarding those who speak out against bullied individuals

B Questions for Discussion

次の 1.~3. の質問について「自分がもっとも同意できる考え」を選択肢 A.~D. より選び、選択した理由を具体的に述べなさい。

1. Will bullying ever end?

   A. No. There will always be bullying. It is a part of human nature.
   B. Yes, but only by making efforts at all levels of society, not just at schools.
   C. Yes. Thinking it cannot be prevented only leads to more and more cases.
   D. Yes, but only in small areas. The world is too big to prevent bullying altogether.

   ....
   ....
   ....

2. How should schools punish students who are found guilty of bullying?

   A. They should be removed from school. This will teach other students not to bully.
   B. Suspension for one year. This will also prevent others from bullying.
   C. Counseling. People who bully can be changed for the better.
   D. Physical punishment of some type. Those who bully should learn how it feels to be bullied themselves.

   Notes: Suspension「停学」

   ....
   ....
   ....

3. What is the best way to escape being bullied?

   A. Communicate well with parents and teachers.
   B. Learn how to defend oneself. Push back when pushed.
   C. Just bear it. All things end, including the years at school.
   D. Stay at home and study via the Internet.

   ....
   ....
   ....

Typical Expressions for Communication:

感じたこと、思ったことを伝えよう⑩

〈「主語の意志」を表す表現〉

will:

I'll talk about this particular subject later.
　（この課題についてはあとで話しましょう。）

prefer to do:

I prefer to talk about solutions rather than problems.
　（問題点よりも解決策について話したい。）

be willing to do:

I'm willing to discuss it and answer questions.
　（それについて話し合って、質問に答えても構いません。）

want to do:

I want to talk about poverty in Japan.
　（日本の貧困について話したい。）

UNIT 11
Armed Conflicts and Refugees

人類の歴史は、戦いの歴史ともいえる。そして、戦争・紛争の犠牲者は、常に弱い者、子ども、女性、そして老人などである。戦争・紛争が起きるとき、家族と自分を守るために数多くの難民が発生する。こうした難民を生み出さないような国同士の外交的努力が必要なのは言うまでもないが、難民受け入れをその社会の活力にするという方法を考えていくことも必要なのかもしれない。

Pre-Study: Words & Phrases

line
1 **warfare**「戦争、武力紛争」
2 **ongoing armed conflicts**「進行中の武力紛争」
表 **cumulative fatalities**「累積死亡者数」
　Afghanistan conflict「アフガニスタン紛争」(1978年以降、アフガニスタンを舞台に断続的に起こっているさまざまな戦闘の総称。)
　Mexican Drug War「メキシコ麻薬戦争」(麻薬組織(カルテル)同士の縄張り争い、および麻薬密売の取締を推進するメキシコ政府と麻薬カルテルとの間で進行中の武力紛争。)
　Syrian Civil War「シリア内戦」(シリアで2011年に起きたシリア政府軍とシリアの反体制派及びそれらの同盟組織などによる内戦。)
　Yemeni Crisis「イエメン危機」(2015年からイエメンで進行中の内戦。ハディ暫定政権をサウジアラビアが、イスラム教シーア派系武装組織フーシをイランが支援し、戦闘が続いている。)
12 **military equipment**「軍装備品」(ここでは「武器」と同じ意味。)
20 **flee from**「〜から逃れる、去る」
20 **refugees and immigrants**「難民と移民」
21 **the United Nations High Commissioner for Refugees**「国連難民高等弁務官事務所」(国際連合が設立した難民保護機関。1990年〜2000年に日本の緒方貞子が高等弁務官を務めた。)
22 **people forcibly displaced**「強制的に追い出される人びと」
27 **the places to which they have evacuated**「人びとが避難した地域」
28 **ill-equipped**「設備が整っていない」
29 **be relocated to**「〜に移住する」
30 **are currently confronting**「目下〜に直面している」

UNIT 11

Human history might be called the history of warfare. The table below presents ongoing armed conflicts that have resulted in the deaths of ten thousand people or more over the past two years. These conflicts include the war in Afghanistan, the civil war in Syria, the crisis in Yemen and the drug war in Mexico. In the same time period, there have been numerous other conflicts that have caused the deaths of between one to ten thousand people. A great many people have died in the past two years alone.

Major Wars (10,000 or more deaths in the current or past year)

Start of conflict	Conflict	Location	Cumulative fatalities	Fatalities in 2018	Fatalities in 2019
1978	Afghanistan conflict	Afghanistan	1,240,000–2,000,000	35,941+	41,735
2006	Mexican Drug War	Mexico	115,000	22,500	17,608
2011	Syrian Civil War	Syria	~570,000	23,000	8,472
2011	Yemeni Crisis	Yemen; Saudi Arabia	60,223–83,700	25,705	20,882

Source: ウィキペディア「進行中の武力紛争のリスト」を基に作成（一部削除）

Data from 2018 shows that the United States is the clear leader in terms of arms sales, with income totaling about 10.5 billion dollars. Russia ranks second with sales of 6.4 billion dollars, with the top five rounded out by France (1.8 billion dollars), Germany (1.3 billion dollars) and Spain (1.2 billion dollars), with South Korea and China also selling more than one billion dollars of military equipment. Saudi Arabia is the number one purchaser of such goods, buying 3.8 billion dollars' worth in 2018. Data from that same year lists other leading purchasers as Australia (1.6 billion dollars), China (also 1.6 billion dollars), and India (1.5 billion dollars). Japan ranks in eleventh place.

The most common victims of war are individuals with the least power: women, children, the aged and the weak. If caught in an area of conflict, the only defense for such people is to escape. In large-scale, prolonged conflicts, people often risk their lives to flee from their homelands, resulting in refugees and immigrants. In 2017, the United Nations High Commissioner for Refugees calculated that the number of people forcibly displaced by armed conflicts numbered around 68.5 million.

The United Nations has proposed three solutions to the problem of world refugees. First, if peace should come to their homelands, refugees should return to the countries of their origins. Yet, conflicts may take years before being resolved. Additional time might then be needed to repair infrastructure and inflation issues. The second solution calls for refugees to remain in the places to which they have evacuated. Yet, those places may be ill-equipped to handle large numbers of people. The third solution calls for refugees to be relocated to other lands. The United States and European countries are currently confronting various problems caused by the flow of refugees. While diplomacy is needed to prevent the emergence of more refugees, how to welcome refugees into a new society remains a critical issue.   (412 words: Not counting the table)

Exercises

A Comprehension Questions

1. According to the table, which armed conflict has caused the second most deaths in the last two years?

   A. The Mexican Drug War
   B. The conflict in Afghanistan
   C. The civil war in Syria
   D. The crisis in Yemen

2. Which country ranks high as both an exporter and importer of military goods?

   A. Japan
   B. Saudi Arabia
   C. China
   D. The United States

3. According to the text, how many war-related refugees were there in 2017?

   A. Over 68 million
   B. More than 10,000 that year
   C. 10.5 billion
   D. 68.5 million in Europe alone

UNIT 11

4. Which of the following is NOT one of the United Nations recommended solutions to the refugee problem?

    A. Return refugees to their homelands
    B. Use diplomacy to stop all refugees
    C. Resettle refugees in other lands
    D. Welcome refugees in the land of their arrival

B Questions for Discussion

次の 1. ~ 3. の質問について「自分がもっとも同意できる考え」を選択肢 A. ~ D. より選び、選択した理由を具体的に述べなさい。

1. How might weapon-producing nations help limit armed conflicts?

    A. They can refuse to sell any more military goods.
    B. They can increase prices so that only wealthy nations can afford weapons.
    C. They can use profits from arms sales to help those harmed by wars.
    D. They can place a limit on how many weapons they sell.

    ....
    ....
    ....

2. What is the biggest problem in accepting refugees from other lands?

    A. Such refugees may include terrorists in their midst.
    B. Refugees cannot understand the language and culture of their new home.
    C. Refugees will take economic opportunities away from other residents of their new home.
    D. Refugees will cause an increase in crime.

    ....
    ....
    ....

3. What can individuals do to help refugees?

   A. Nothing. Refugees are not welcome and need to return to their homelands.
   B. They can economically sponsor individual refugees or refugee families.
   C. They can volunteer to teach refugees language or customs.
   D. They can help find employment for refugees.

   ....
   ....
   ....

Typical Expressions for Communication:
感じたこと、思ったことを伝えよう⑪

〈「理由・原因」を表す表現〉

because:
It was called the Cold War because there was no active war between the two nations.
　(それはCold Warと呼ばれた。なぜなら、その２つの国のあいだで実際の戦争があったわけではないので。)

as:
As you were out, I left a message.
　(きみが外出中だったので、私はメッセージを残しました。)

due to:
The team's recent victory was largely due to his efforts.
　(チームの最近の勝利は、おもに彼の働きのせいだった。)

thanks to:
The success of our project is thanks to the hard work of the company's staff.
　(我々のプロジェクトの成功は、会社のスタッフが懸命に働いてくれたおかげだ。)

UNIT 12
Food Waste

食品ロスとは、売れ残りや食べ残し、期限切れの食品など、本来は食べることのできる食品を廃棄することで、世界的な問題になっている。一方で、World Food Programme (WFP) の報告によると、世界には飢餓や栄養不足に苦しむ人々が約 8 億 2 千万人、世界人口の 9 人に一人が飢えに苦しんでいるという。各国はさまざまな対策が必要だが、日本では食品ロスの半分は家庭で発生するので、個人個人も真剣に取り組まなければならない。

Pre-Study: Words & Phrases

line
1 **food discarded**「廃棄された食品」
3 **expiration date**「賞味期限」
3 **the Food and Agriculture Organization of the United Nations**「国連食糧農業機関」
4 **the Ministry of Agriculture, Forestry and Fisheries**「農林水産省」
5 **assessed ... at**「(金額・損害など) を〜と査定した」
9 **be destroyed prior to harvest**「収穫前にダメになる」
9 **pest infestations**「害虫の侵入」
12 **at the retail level**「小売段階での」
13 **be tossed away**「廃棄される」
14 **unsightly appearance or shape**「見た目の悪い姿や形」
17 **the World Food Programme**「国連世界食糧計画 (WFP)」(食糧欠乏国と天災などの被災国に食糧援助を行う国際連合の機関。)
19 **malnutrition**「栄養不足」
21 **not to mention families**「家庭は言うまでもない」
24 **garbage dumps**「ごみ処理場」
26 **Sustainable Development Goals**「持続可能な開発目標：SDGs」(2015 年 9 月の国連総会で採択された「持続可能な開発のための 2030 アジェンダ」で掲げられている「貧困の解消」「環境保全」など 17 の目標と 169 の達成基準から成る。)
29 **meet this goal**「この目標を達成する」

Food Waste

45 Food waste has become a global problem. Such waste includes food discarded because it has not been sold, food left uneaten, or food aged past the recommended expiration date. The Food and Agriculture Organization of the United Nations estimates that 1.3 billion tons of edible food are thrown away every year. In 2016, the Ministry of Agriculture, Forestry and Fisheries assessed the annual amount of discarded food in Japan at nearly 6.5 million tons per year. This means each person in Japan is responsible for roughly 51 kilograms of food waste each year.

46 There are numerous factors that influence food waste. For example, crops might be destroyed prior to harvest by pest infestations or severe weather, or if not destroyed, they might not reach acceptable standards of quality. Food might also be discarded during the processing stage. Stored food might be spoiled by pests or damaged in some other way due to inadequate storage. There is food waste at the retail level as well, where food may be tossed away due to over-purchasing, the passing of recommended expiration dates, or unsightly appearance or shape. Consumers are also big wasters of food. They buy too much, leave amounts uneaten, store items improperly, and ruin food during the cooking process.

47 Food resources are limited and discarded food is a waste of resources. In 2018, the World Food Programme estimated that 820 million people are suffering from hunger or malnutrition, approximately one out of every nine people on earth. Such a number highlights the enormous waste of 1.3 billion tons of food each year. Food waste also results in financial losses by food producers, not to mention families. Raw materials and production have costs, with another large expense being the management of waste materials. Food waste damages the environment as well. The processing of garbage dumps emits large amounts of carbon dioxide, which in turn contributes to global warming.

48 In 2015, the United Nations announced seventeen Sustainable Development Goals. The second goal on the list is to eliminate world hunger. The objective is to end hunger and improve nutrition through a stable supply of food, with a target year of 2030. Each country is taking various measures to help meet this goal. Production companies are extending expiration dates and freshness retention for food and food banks are garnering more support from the public. Individuals should strive not to order too much when eating out, and to take home leftover food. Families should store food carefully and neither purchase nor prepare more than they can use. Half of

the food waste in Japan originates in the home, meaning that each individual needs to consider their food habits seriously. (444 words)

Exercises

A Comprehension Questions

1. How much food is wasted in Japan each year?

    A. 51 kilograms
    B. 6.5 million tons
    C. 1.3 million tons
    D. 1.3 billion tons

2. How do stores waste food?

    A. By leaving food uneaten
    B. By buying too much
    C. By spoiling food during the cooking process
    D. By discarding food during the processing stage

3. According to the text, how many people are suffering from hunger in the world?

    A. Nine million
    B. 1.3 billion
    C. One out of every 820 million
    D. Close to one billion

4. According to the passage, which of the following is one way for an individual to help end world hunger?

    A. By extending expiration dates on food
    B. By avoiding food with unsightly appearance or shape
    C. By contributing food to food banks
    D. By killing insects and other pests

B Questions for Discussion

次の 1.～3. の質問について「自分がもっとも同意できる考え」を選択肢 A.～D. より選び、選択した理由を具体的に述べなさい。

1. What is an effective way to help lessen world hunger?

    A. Stay slim. Maintain a strict diet.
    B. Purchase only necessary food items.
    C. Ship food to needy areas.
    D. Volunteer at a food bank.

    ....
    ....
    ....

2. Should a person eat food beyond the expiration date?

    A. Yes, the date is only a recommendation.
    B. Never. Companies have responsibility to provide fresh food.
    C. No. Such food should be shipped to needy areas.
    D. Only if stores first reduce the price.

    ....
    ....
    ....

3. How might Japan lower its total of 6.5 million tons of wasted food per year?

    A. Rotate crops so that the harvest time does not conflict with the typhoon season.
    B. Increase fees for garbage pickup.
    C. Limit the number of restaurants and convenience stores.
    D. Conduct seminars on food management at schools.

    ....
    ....
    ....

UNIT 12

Typical Expressions for Communication:
感じたこと、思ったことを伝えよう⑫

〈「時」に関する接続詞〉

when:
You should strive not to order too much when eating out.
（外食するときには注文しすぎないように努めるべきである。）

before:
You should not interrupt other speakers before they finish.
（他の人が話し終わる前にさえぎってはいけない。）

while:
People need to plan for their old age while (they are) still young.
（人はまだ若いうちに年を取ったときのために計画を立てる必要がある。）

after:
Many Chinese tourists visited Kenya after China made Kenya one of its tourist destinations.
（中国がケニアを旅行目的地の一つにした後、多くの中国人がケニアを訪れた。）

UNIT 13
Future Energy

エネルギー資源とは、産業、運輸、そして私たちの生活に必要な動力の源で、現在、多くの国では石炭、石油などの化石燃料を使用している。だが、一方で、化石燃料は、地球温暖化やプラスチックの海洋汚染などを引き起こし、地球規模の問題の源となっている。こうした問題を解決する未来のエネルギーとして研究が進められているのが水素発電と核融合発電である。

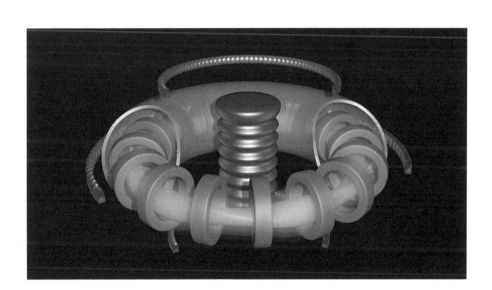

Pre-Study: Words & Phrases

line
- 2 **fossil fuels**「化石燃料」
- 4 **microplastic pollution**「マイクロプラスチック汚染」
- 6 **renewable energy**「再生可能エネルギー」
- 9 **detergents**「洗剤」
- 10 **the Institute for Sustainable Energy Policies**「環境エネルギー政策研究所」
- 13 **Basic Energy Plan**「エネルギー基本計画」
- 17 **additional flaw**「付随した欠陥」
- 19 **hydrogen power**「水素発電」
- 21 **for generating electric energy**「電気エネルギーを発生させるために」
- 23 **electrolysis**「電気分解」
- 26 **nuclear fusion**「核融合発電」
- 27 **fuse hydrogen atoms**「水素原子を融合させる」
- 28 **not attainable at present**「現在は実現できていない」

UNIT 13

🎧 49 Energy resources provide power for industry, transportation, and—of course—our daily lives. At present, most nations depend on fossil fuels for energy, including oil, coal, and natural gas. Yet, use of such fuels has brought about world-wide environmental problems, such as global warming and the microplastic pollution of the seas. Faced with this situation, every nation is now expanding development of alternative energies. Let's look at some of these options, including renewable energy sources such as nuclear power, solar power and wind power, and the nuclear fusion dream option.

🎧 50 Fossil fuels are used not only as energy for airplanes and automobiles, but also as a raw material in plastic and detergents. They also play a large role in the production of electricity at electric power plants. In the case of Japan, the Institute for Sustainable Energy Policies states that, in 2018, fossil fuels provided 78% of Japanese electric power production, with the remaining 22% from non-fossil fuel sources. According to the "Basic Energy Plan" announced by the Japanese government in 2018, by the year 2030, Japan hopes to reduce this 78% total to 56%, with the remaining amount to come from nuclear energy (between 20 and 22%) and other renewable energy sources (between 22 and 24%). Yet this plan fails to eliminate the production of carbon dioxide and has the additional flaw of creating nuclear waste materials.

Source	Ratio	Source	Ratio
Coal	28.3%	Hydro	7.8%
LNG	37.4%	Solar	6.5%
Oil	3.7%	Wind	0.7%
Other Thermal	8.5%	Biomass	2.2%
Nuclear	4.7%	Geothermal	0.2%

Power supply mix of Japan (2018)

Source: ISEP based on data of METI

 51 The future energy source that is developing most rapidly is hydrogen power. Hydrogen power uses hydrogen and oxygen found in the atmosphere as a fuel source for generating electric energy. It produces no carbon dioxide and is considered a very clean energy source. At present, most hydrogen comes from fossil fuels, but if hydrogen can be produced through electrolysis using some form of renewable energy, then no carbon dioxide will be created. High costs may prevent the use of clean hydrogen power by 2030, but by 2040 the cost problems will most likely be solved.

Nuclear fusion is the most sought-after of all energy sources. Nuclear fusion uses high temperatures to fuse hydrogen atoms and, unlike other forms of nuclear power, produces no nuclear waste. Nuclear fusion is not attainable at present, but scientists feel it might be workable by 2050. The world and Japan have serious energy concerns, yet they must be solved. People have always risen to meet the needs of tomorrow.

(392 words)

Exercises

A. Comprehension Questions

1. What problems have the use of fossil fuels created?

   A. The development of alternative energy sources
   B. Global environmental concerns
   C. Insufficient energy for industry and transportation
   D. Inferior plastics and detergents

2. By the year 2030, by how much does Japan hope to reduce its dependency on fossil fuels in the creation of electric energy?

   A. By 22%
   B. By 78%
   C. Between 20 and 22%
   D. Between 22 and 24%

3. What is the chief advantage of hydrogen power produced by electrolysis made by some renewable energy source?

   A. It uses oxygen found in the air.
   B. It creates no nuclear waste.
   C. It does not produce carbon dioxide.
   D. It is cost free.

UNIT 13

4. Why is nuclear fusion considered a "dream" energy source?

   A. Nuclear fusion is absolutely impossible.

   B. It produces no nuclear waste.

   C. It requires almost no fossil fuel.

   D. It will reverse global warming.

B Questions for Discussion

次の1.～3.の質問について「自分がもっとも同意できる考え」を選択肢 A.～D. より選び、選択した理由を具体的に述べなさい。

1. What is the best way for individuals to help limit energy costs?

   A. By using public transportation and walking whenever possible

   B. By avoiding plastic products and using natural detergents

   C. By avoiding use of air conditioners and heaters whenever possible

   D. By working or studying from home and not commuting to a specific work place or educational institution

   ....
   ....
   ....

2. What is the best approach toward electric energy produced by nuclear power plants?

   A. Such plants are dangerous and must be stopped at once.

   B. Such plants are necessary now, but must be replaced as soon as workable alternatives are developed.

   C. The public reaction to such plants is exaggerated. Those power plants should continue as they are.

   D. The use of such plants should be expanded. Japan, as an isolated island nation, badly needs its own energy.

   ....
   ....
   ....

3. Which possible renewable energy source might best fit Japan?

   A. Solar energy. Japan has clear skies much of the year, including hot summers. If this energy can be stored, it is best.
   B. Geothermal energy. This energy comes from the earth and Japan is rich in volcanoes and hot springs. This energy fits Japan.
   C. Wind power. As an island nation, Japan has lots of coastline, which might serve as good locations for wind turbines.
   D. Hydroelectric power. This uses energy created by rivers and dams. Japan has a good water supply, so this method matches well.

   ....
   ....
   ....

Typical Expressions for Communication:
感じたこと、思ったことを伝えよう⑬

〈「説得・提案・助言」を表す表現〉

suggest:
What steps would you suggest to reduce energy consumption?
　（エネルギーの消費を減らすために、どのような手順を提案しますか？）

advise:
The police have advised all drivers to place chains on their tires, due to the snowstorm.
　（吹雪のため、警察はすべてのドライバーに対し、タイヤにチェーンを装着するように警告した。）

recommend:
The doctor has recommended that smokers stop using e-cigarette products.
　（医者は喫煙者は電子タバコ製品の使用をやめるべきだと忠告した。）

propose:
The EPA has proposed that existing plants reduce carbon emissions by 30 percent.
　（環境保護庁は既存の工場に炭素の排出を30パーセント減らすよう提案した。）

UNIT 14
Medical Care in the Future

人間は生まれた瞬間から老化が始まり、病気と死は避けることができない。だが、医療分野における進歩には目覚ましいものがあり、これまでは一旦発病すると治療が困難だったり、必ず死に至る病気だったもののなかには、がんをはじめ未来には克服されるものがある。こうした医学的前進の結果、人間の寿命も21世紀半ばぐらいには150歳に延びるという予測もある。

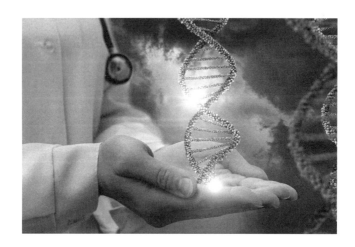

Pre-Study: Words & Phrases

line
- 4 **dementia**「認知症」
- 7 **life-threatening**「生命を脅かす」
- 9 **the Global Burden of Disease Study**「世界疾病負担 (GBD)」(世界保健機関 (WHO) などが行っている研究の名称。病気の危険因子、死亡率などを研究するプログラム。)
- 13 **cancerous genes**「がん遺伝子」
- 14 **cancer will be detected**「がんが発見されるようになる」
- 16 **nanoparticles**「ナノ粒子」($1 \sim 100$ nm (ナノメートル；10^{-9} m) 程度の大きさを有する粒子。nano は「10億分の1」を意味する。)
- 17 **may not be eliminated**「根絶できないかもしれない」
- 18 **a fatal illness**「死病」
- 18 **no more threatening than the common cold**「風邪と同じように怖いものでない」
- 20 **regenerative medicine**「再生医療」
- 22 **induced pluripotent stem cells**「人工多能性幹細胞 (iPS 細胞)」
- 24 **various tissues and organs**「さまざまな組織や臓器」
- 29 **diabetes**「糖尿病」
- 29 **remedies for rheumatism**「リウマチの治療法」
- 31 **self-worth and happiness**「自分に価値を認めることや幸福」

Medical Care in the Future

🎧 53　The aging process begins the moment people are born. There is no way for anyone to escape sickness and death. At present one out of every two people will die of cancer and it is said that over forty-six million people around the world have some form of dementia. People suffer from a wide range of serious conditions, including heart disease and stroke. At the same time, medical science is making remarkable advances. Illnesses that untill now have been almost impossible to treat and others that are currently thought to bring about certain death will perhaps not be life-threatening in the future.

🎧 54　According to the Global Burden of Disease Study, in 2017, there were 17.2 million cancer patients world-wide, with 8.9 million deaths by cancer. Yet, due to the rise of medical technology, the number of cancer patients will level off by the year 2050, with almost no one under age eighty dying of cancer. This will be the result of advanced analysis of cancerous genes and the mapping of what types of such genes each person might possess. In the future, cancer will be detected at a very early stage, allowing for successful treatment before it progresses. Even if detected at a later stage, the cancer of the future will be treated by anti-cancer agents using nanoparticles that will cause almost no damage to healthy cells. Cancer may not be eliminated, but it may no longer be considered a fatal illness. People may consider it no more threatening than the common cold.

🎧 55　Regenerative medicine also holds hope for the future. Such an approach uses the body's own cells and regenerative powers. Research in this area has only recently begun, but the induced pluripotent stem cells (iPS cells) developed by Professor Shinya Yamanaka of Kyoto University are renowned. Such IPS cells can be applied to restore various tissues and organs. No one knows the future, but some predict that by the year 2045, scientists will be able to recreate most organs in the laboratory. The time may be coming when we can replace body organs that have become ineffective due to disease or old age.

🎧 56　Many other medical processes are also advancing, including anti-aging measures, cures for diabetes, the creation of artificial blood, and remedies for rheumatism. By the mid-21st century, the human lifespan may approach 150 years. In such a future, mankind's bigger problems might be mental health and the search for self-worth and happiness.

(406 words)

UNIT 14

Exercises

A Comprehension Questions

1. How many people in the world now will die of cancer?

   A. One out of every two
   B. 46 million
   C. 17.2 million
   D. 8.3 million

2. According to the text, will cancer disappear in the future?

   A. Yes, it will disappear by 2050.
   B. Yes, if detected at an early stage.
   C. No, but it will no longer be considered dangerous.
   D. No, but it will only affect people aged eighty or older.

3. According to the text, what might regenerative medicine be able to do in the future?

   A. Recreate humans in the laboratory
   B. Replace people's bodies
   C. Make new organs in the laboratory
   D. Make iPS cell research ineffective

4. According to the text, what might become a more serious human health concern in the future?

   A. Rheumatism
   B. The aging process
   C. Psychological issues
   D. Problems with medical ethics

B Questions for Discussion

次の 1.～3. の質問について「自分がもっとも同意できる考え」を選択肢 A.～D. より選び、選択した理由を具体的に述べなさい。

1. What do you think would be the biggest problem with a human lifespan of 150 years?

   A. Finding some way to fill all the additional time
   B. Finding adequate living space and food for all the extra people
   C. Maintaining good relationships with others over all those years
   D. Finding ways to live even longer when the 150 years ends

   ....
   ....
   ....

2. Might the creation of human organs in a laboratory be considered improper?

   A. Yes, it puts scientists in the position of creator or god.
   B. Yes, it will create a market for life-saving organs that only the wealthy will be able to afford.
   C. No, it will save lives and that is the goal of medicine.
   D. No, it can be controlled by the government and monitoring agencies.

   ....
   ....
   ....

3. What is the ideal human lifespan?

   A. As long as possible
   B. Long enough to see one's children settled and successful
   C. Long enough to do all the things a person wants to do
   D. It doesn't matter. When your time comes, it comes.

   ....
   ....
   ....

UNIT 14

Typical Expressions for Communication:
感じたこと、思ったことを伝えよう⑭

〈「禁止・警告」の表現〉

prohibit:
Our Privacy Policy prohibits us from accepting users who are under the age of 18 years.
　（当社のプライバシーに関する方針により、18歳以下の利用者をお引き受けすることはできません。）

forbid:
School rules forbid smartphone usage in the classroom.
　（校則によって教室でのスマートホンの使用は禁止されている。）

warn:
Local authorities have warned tourists against hiking and trekking in the village of Hakuba.
　（地元当局は白馬村における旅行者にハイキングとトレッキングをしないように警告した。）

caution:
His doctor cautioned him to take it easy.
　（かかりつけの医者は彼に無理をしないようにと注意した。）

UNIT 15
The Universe in the Future

1969年7月21日、アメリカのアポロ11号の着陸船「イーグル号」が月面に着陸した。以来、人類は宇宙開発において大きな飛躍を続けてきた。かつてはアメリカやソ連が国家として開発してきたが、21世紀に入り、民間企業が宇宙開発事業に参入してきている。その一つ、アメリカのスペースX社は、2024年までに火星に有人宇宙船を送り、その後、火星に都市を建設するという。

Pre-Study: Words & Phrases

line
1 **lunar module Eagle**「月着陸船イーグル号」
2 **heavenly body**「天体（太陽・月など）」
4 **one giant leap for mankind**「人類にとって偉大な跳躍」
9 **an unmanned space probe**「無人宇宙探査機」
12 **the International Space Station**「国際宇宙ステーション (ISS)」
12 **outer space**「宇宙空間」
14 **the Itokawa asteroid**「小惑星イトカワ」
17 **land rover**「ジープに似た四輪駆動 (4WD) 自動車」
18 **a reusable launch vehicle**「再利用型打ち上げロケット」
25 **come into the limelight**「世間の注目を引くようになる」
27 **PayPal**「ペイパル」（インターネットを利用した決済サービス (PayPal) を提供するアメリカの企業。ユーザー数は世界で2億5000万人以上。）
28 **space-bearing civilization and a multi-planet species**「宇宙に生きる文明と（多くの惑星間で繁栄する）多惑星種」
29 **humans still need a Plan B**「人類はそれでもプランB（＝代替案）を必要としている」
29 **…, should the earth become uninhabitable**「もしも地球が住めなくなるなら」
32 **sustain**「を養う、を維持する」

UNIT 15

On July 20, 1969, the Apollo 11 lunar module Eagle landed on the surface of the moon. For the first time in history, people had left Mother Earth for another heavenly body. Captain Neil Armstrong's first words upon stepping out upon the moon's surface are famous: "That's one small step for a man, one giant leap for mankind."

From that moment on, mankind has continued to make more leaps in the development of space exploration. Following are some of the main achievements:

* The first Japanese satellite, "Ohsumi," was successfully launched in 1970.
* The Soviet Union established the first permanent space station in 1971.
* Also in 1971, the Soviet Union successfully landed an unmanned space probe on Mars, the "Venera 7".
* In 1981, the United States successfully launched the first space shuttle, "Columbia".
* In 1998, construction of the International Space Station began in outer space, a joint effort of many nations.
* The Japanese space probe "Hayabusa" successfully landed on the Itokawa asteroid and returned to the earth with samples, a project lasting from 2003 to 2010.
* In 2011, construction of the International Space Station was completed.
* In 2012, America successfully landed "Curiosity," a car-sized land rover, on Mars.
* In 2015, the "Falcon 9 v1.2," a reusable launch vehicle produced by the American private aerospace manufacturer SpaceX, was launched and returned to earth successfully.
* In 2017, SpaceX successfully launched the first reusable spacecraft.
* In 2018, America conducted a full-power experiment for a nuclear power station to be used one day on Mars.

The early era of space exploration was driven by the "Space Race" between the Soviet Union and the United States. Yet, in the 21st century, private firms have come into the limelight for their space development businesses. For example, Elon Musk, the founder of PayPal, began SpaceX in 2002. Musk has stated that mankind will become a "space-bearing civilization and a multi-planet species." He feels it is important to care for the earth's environment, but humans still need a Plan B, should the earth become uninhabitable. Musk plans to launch a manned spacecraft bound for Mars in 2024 and eventually build a colony there. He feels that within forty to one hundred years, the Martian colony could sustain a population of one million people. This dreamlike scenario cannot be completely denied anymore.

The development of space was initially for military purposes and to a large extent this has not changed. Yet at the same time space development is helping improve life on our planet. How we will use the splendid technology of space exploration depends on us.

(439 words)

Exercises

A Comprehension Questions

1. What was the name of the first manned vessel on the moon?

   A. Ohsumi
   B. Eagle
   C. Hayabusa
   D. SpaceX

2. What nation built the International Space Station?

   A. The United States
   B. Russia
   C. Russia and the United States together
   D. Several countries together

3. How soon does Elon Musk think there can be a sustainable colony on Mars?

   A. Approximately before the end of this century
   B. By 2024
   C. Never, it is only a dream.
   D. When the earth becomes uninhabitable

4. What has typically been the primary goal behind space exploration?

   A. The betterment of human life
   B. To study outer space more closely
   C. To increase military might
   D. To colonize Mars

UNIT 15

B Questions for Discussion

次の 1. ~ 3. の質問について「自分がもっとも同意できる考え」を選択肢 A. ~ D. より選び、選択した理由を具体的に述べなさい。

1. Would you volunteer for travel to Mars?

    A. No, it is cirtain to be dangerous.
    B. No, there is no reason to leave the earth.
    C. Yes, the opportunity to be a pioneer is exciting.
    D. Yes, our planet is dying and Mars provides an escape.

    ....
    ....
    ....

2. Do you think that having a colony on Mars within one hundred years is possible?

    A. Yes, technology is progressing rapidly.
    B. Yes, competition between nations and companies will lead the way.
    C. No, the scientific problems are too big.
    D. No, mankind will be destroyed by then.

    ....
    ....
    ....

3. What would be the most difficult thing in leaving Earth for life on Mars?

    A. Leaving behind family and friends, perhaps never to meet again.
    B. Leaving behind common earthly comforts, such as housing and food.
    C. Missing popular entertainment, like music, film and sports.
    D. Giving up all the realities of life on earth for something completely unknown.

    ....
    ....
    ....

Typical Expressions for Communication:
感じたこと、思ったことを伝えよう⑮

〈「条件」の表現〉

if:

If one person listens well and the other does not, communication will fail.
　（もし一人がよく聞いて、もう一人がよく聞かないと、コミュニケーションは上手くいかない。）

in case ...:

We should buy batteries for the flashlight, in case there is a power outage.
　（停電するといけないので、懐中電灯の電池を買ったほうがよい。）

in case of:

In case of fire, use the stairway, not the elevator.
　（火事のときは階段を使用しなさい。エレベーターは駄目です。）

suppose ...:

Suppose something goes wrong. Then what would you do?
　（何かが上手くいかなくなったら、きみはどうする？）

Reading Current Issues
Developing Communication Skills through English

知っておくべき日本と世界の論点・未来の夢

編著者   Tom Dillon
            西 谷 恒 志
発行者   山 口 隆 史

発 行 所   株式会社 音羽書房鶴見書店
〒113-0033 東京都文京区本郷4-1-14
TEL 03-3814-0491
FAX 03-3814-9250
URL: http://www.otowatsurumi.com
e-mail: info@otowatsurumi.com

2020年 3月 1日   初版発行
2020年12月 1日   2 刷発行

組版・装幀   ほんのしろ
印刷・製本   (株)シナノ
■ 落丁・乱丁本はお取り替えいたします。

EC-072